school

WITHDRAWN

D1717074

J. Jean Robertson

Educational Media

rourkeeducationalmedia.com

*Scan for Related Titles
and Teacher Resources*

Teaching Focus:

Endings: -*ies*- Locate the word libraries and activities from the text. Write the word and the root word next to each other. How does the root word change when making it plural, to mean more than one? Review how the letter *y* is changed to *i* before adding –*es*. Practice writing the plural form using other words that end in *y*.

Before Reading:

Building Academic Vocabulary and Background Knowledge

Before reading a book, it is important to set the stage for your child or student by using pre-reading strategies. This will help them develop their vocabulary, increase their reading comprehension, and make connections across the curriculum.

1. *Read the title and look at the cover. Let's make predictions about what this book will be about.*
2. *Take a picture walk by talking about the pictures/photographs in the book. Implant the vocabulary as you take the picture walk. Be sure to talk about the text features such as headings, the Table of Contents, glossary, bolded words, captions, charts/diagrams, or index.*
3. *Have students read the first page of text with you then have students read the remaining text.*
4. *Strategy Talk – use to assist students while reading.*
   - Get your mouth ready
   - Look at the picture
   - Think…does it make sense
   - Think…does it look right
   - Think…does it sound right
   - Chunk it – by looking for a part you know
5. *Read it again.*
6. *After reading the book, complete the activities below.*

Content Area Vocabulary
Use glossary words in a sentence.

Cyrillic
equator
homeschooled
library buses
private schools
public schools

After Reading:

Comprehension and Extension Activity

After reading the book, work on the following questions with your child or students in order to check their level of reading comprehension and content mastery.

1. *How are schools in the countries from the book similar to yours? How are they different? (Text to self connection)*
2. *What are some ways students get information? (Summarize)*
3. *What types of games do you and your friends play at recess? (Text to self connection)*
4. *Why is having computers in schools important? (Asking questions)*

Extension Activity

Schools across the world all have the same focus: To teach students. But they have many differences and similarities to your school. Select another country that is not in the book and research things about the schools there. How long is a school day? What types of foods are served at lunch? Do they study different things than you? What language do they use? Then create a Venn diagram to display the similarities and differences between your school and the one you researched.

How are schools alike? How are they different?

Skipping rope games are popular playground activities at schools in England. Children there begin school at age five and must stay in school until they are 16.

North
America

South
America

England

Europe

Africa

Asia

Australia

North America

South America

Europe

Africa

Asia

China

Australia

School begins at 7:30 a.m. and ends at 5 p.m. in China. They have a two hour lunch break. Chinese schools have one computer for every two students.

North America

Europe

Asia

Africa

South America

Australia

Australian children enjoy playing handball at recess. There is one computer for every three students in their classrooms.

Iran has many schools that do not have libraries. **Library buses**, with about 3,000 books each, visit these schools.

Boys and girls learn in separate classes in Iran and other places in the Middle East.

equator

North America

Europe

Asia

Brazil

Africa

South America

Australia

Students in Brazil have summer vacation in December and January, because Brazil is south of the **equator**.

Students in Russia bundle up in warm clothes during the winter. Russians use an alphabet called **Cyrillic**.

In Kenya, many people go hungry. Some students save the lunch they are given at school to take home to their families.

North America
Europe
Asia
Africa
Israel
South America
Australia

Children in Israel speak and read Hebrew.

Their language reads from right to left.

School is different in each state in the United States. Some children go to **public schools**, some go to **private schools**, and some are **homeschooled**.

What is school like for you?

Photo Glossary

 **Cyrillic** (si-RI-lik): An alphabet used for writing many eastern European and Asian languages.

 **equator** (i-KWAY-tur): An imaginary line around the center of the Earth, dividing the Northern Hemisphere from the Southern Hemisphere.

 **homeschooled** (HOME-SKOOLD): Children who are taught school at home.